Enchantment & Other Demons

Other Books by Ron Smith

The Silver Fox
Rainshadow (Edited with Stephen Guppy)
Seasonal
A Buddha Named Baudelaire

Enchantment
& Other Demons

poems by

Ron Smith

oolichan books

LANTZVILLE / BRITISH COLUMBIA /CANADA
1995

Canadian Cataloguing in Publication Data

Smith, Ron, 1943-

Enchantment and other demons

ISBN 0-88982-152-6

I. Title.

PS8587.M5838E52 1995   C811'.54   C95-910862-9

PR9199.3.S64E52 1995

Publication of this book has been financially assisted by The Canada Council.

Published by
oolichan books
P.O. Box 10
Lantzville, B.C.
Canada V0R 2H0

Printed in Canada by
Morriss Printing Company
Victoria, B.C.

For Robert Kroetsch

and

To the Memory of Dick Morriss
and
Morris Donaldson

And, as always, for Pat

Acknowledgements

The author wishes to thank the editors of the following magazines and anthologies in which some of the poems from this collection first appeared: *The Canadian Forum*; *The Moosehead Anthology*; *Towards 2000*; *Skookum Wawa*; *Transcript* (England); *Atrevida*; *The Capilano Review*; *The Camrose Review*; *Island* (Australia); *Vintage 93*; *Nimrod* (U.S.A.); *Forum* (Jugoslavia); *Meanjin* (Australia); and *Matrix*.

The "Nicole" poems in Part Two were collected in the chapbook, *Seasonal*, published in 1984 by Sono Nis Press, Victoria, B.C. A broadside of "Owen: December 22" was published in a limited edition of fifty by Morriss Printing and Oolichan Books in 1987.

Another version of the long prose poem, *Arabesque*, appeared in book form as *A Buddha Named Baudelaire* with Sono Nis Press in 1988.

Thanks to Diane Einblau whose compassion as well as lines and notes provided the inspiration for Section 1 of "Fires of Chernobyl."

And for their help with this book the author wishes to thank Edwin Webb, Jay Connolly, Joe Rosenblatt, Steve Guppy, Rhonda Bailey, Gary Geddes, Pat Smith and several friends who generously read earlier drafts of some of the poems, as well as to B.C. Cultural Services for its financial support in 1991, when a number of these poems were written.

Contents

Things As They Are

Seasonal

Enchantment & Other Demons

Arabesque

1

Things As They Are

The Abundance of Being

He spoke, kept speaking, of God
    — Wallace Stevens

How you want us to struggle with the tortured
and twisted roots of imagination. An old stump

tossed onto the beach. Gnarled insight. A dance
of old bones. How easy it is to condemn or

chastise, to overlook the slender columbine and
climbing wisteria in the spring garden when

we have left the cold winds and snow behind.
Should we lament the change of seasons, abandon

what we have longed for from a distance —
fresh winds and clear mountain streams. Our lives

are in siege. The politics of this place
condemn each of us to boredom. Empty houses,

vacant lots, supermarkets, asphalt. The earth
is dying, consumed by the thousands of fires

we have lit with our own hands. Arsonists
to the stars. Smoke stacks stand like monuments

to our supplication. Rain falls from our eyes.
What have we become? Here we breathe our last breath

beneath a canopy of night, and marvel at the sculptor's
block of stone. The pale horse of discordant dreams

rides the night sky as if pursued by our desire
to leap holy and willy-nilly into the heavens.

Under Snow

When the world lies under snow
and all other sounds are muffled
I hear earthworms tunnel
beneath the crusty soil —
hush, listen closely
to these phantom steps of spring.

At this moment we should not speak
of dying, for our time has been
short enough, the measure of a few degrees
between seasons.
          I shall bury my thoughts
in the rot of delicate blooms. I shall embrace
the sanctity of decay,
a joy born of compost.

Mud dries on my winter boots
and shadows cast by hearth fires grow dim.

Do not lament the dead.
Do not be startled when snow
drifts across the doors of empty houses
and ice floes thicken.

A new language will follow the fractured earth,
the rising sun. A fresh sky will open
as earthworms survey their domain.

Horizons

for Edwin

Understand, what follows was meant to happen:
At low tide, a brisk wind blows down the bay,
a northwesterly, the good weather wind.
A small boat, sparkling white and top heavy
glides before the swelling sea. A man,
standing in the cockpit, glances at the
August sun and wipes sweat from his forehead.
His arms motion, back and forth, and
from where I stand, ankle deep in kelp,
I wave back, wondering if he signals for help.
I long to speak as the gaze of the world
fills with the blue of sea and sky — horizons
blur. I want to tell him that heaven
touches the earth and all are safe.

But the boat heaves and lurches as it slides
past Maude Island, into open water, and
begins to yaw. Above me a kite flutters,
dips, rises nervously, tearing the wind.
A clamshell, nudged toward shore, bumps
against my foot. Farther out in the strait,
the boat plunges down a slope, from crest
to trough. Stern high, the propeller rises
out of the water; I hear the engine
race; the rudder lifts, loses its grip,
the sea taking charge. The man hauls

on the tiller but the vessel slips
sideways until only the top of the cabin
is visible. Soon this man, who followed
his compass into my life, vanishes
in the movement of sea and wind and memory.

The surf pounds in my blood and the distance
between us is broken. Now I understand
the horizon, the limits of love that circle
and bind us. Somewhere out of the blue
he has landed and people welcome him.
Or, he's still falling, gracefully, through
celestial dust, pulled by the beasts of fury
into the shadows. Sometimes, when the world
appears to be flat and light dims in our eyes,
there are dark passages to our thoughts.

The tide swirls around my feet; I watch
the kite cut a brilliant red hole in the sky.
This is one of those days, one of those
beautiful days, when it's possible
to be pitched off the edge of the world.
I shout, Over there, over there,
I saw a man and his boat disappear —
but no one sees.

And Still We Continue Dreaming

Past midnight, in the moon's dead light,
the earth moans, the December sea recedes,
rolling into dreams and memories of morning.

Nothing changes. What are we to believe?
The still eye of winter storms? At dawn
the sky clouds over, mists veil the garden.

We listen for sermons from the swirling rain
as if they might reveal stories from the past.
How slowly we note what is worthy of praise.

We look blindly for disaster, measure
each leafless tree, weigh each winter's havoc
against the calligraphy of summer.

We are born into words. What else do we need
to bring reverence to our hearts? Sand dollars
stand on edge to feed, their survival

an economy of purpose. Gulls surf the sky
on sudden gusts of cold air. Your fingers
brush my cheek; I feel the invisible

wings of snow. The world is a grey place
without these dreams that soar within us;
that climb into the everlasting, naked blue.

Ten Firs

for Joe Rosenblatt

Every time we walk past these giant firs
you stretch out your hand
to feel the contours of rough bark.
You reach in, touch the rings of life
and brood over our loss of grace,
an emptiness at the circle's centre,
where heart, branches, roots once merged.

Your hand slips from the trunk. Priest
of tall trees, you mumble a blessing,
a gentle, gruff song, and we carry on
shuffling down the road. You —
your back bent with the weight of the tree
that grows within — accept this gift, fearful
the path we follow is enclosed in night
and dawn won't ripen one more time
to consecrate this glorious burst of green.

Dogs at Night

Out of the ebb and flow of dreams
I hear the distant rush of the sea
wash, wave after wave, across tidal
flats. Wind catches in the trees, lazy
and monotonous, keening in the night.
But it is the sound of dogs barking
that stirs me from my bed. I get up,
stumble to the kitchen and look out,
through binoculars, into the moonlight,
see black forms circle and recoil from
a shape half submerged in a tidal pool.

The frantic yelp of dogs pushes
against the wind. I'm drawn to their
cries, but equally back to my bed.

I imagine it is a body they snap at
and nuzzle up to. I'm easily
influenced by the news, unsolved
mysteries, documentaries, all
that blurs in this sordid world. Or
is this a dream wounded by distractions
from out there, blood stirred and teased
by the scent of a frightened animal?

Language is biological. Howls
become lyrical and rapturous,
and a chorus line of lights flashes on
up and down the beach, then as quickly,
turns off, my neighbours whispering back
to bed. I imagine they bury
their faces in pillows, sink back
into blissful dreams. But harm continues
to pester my thoughts. I put away
the glasses, sit in the rocker by
the window and focus on the roll
of the sea. Possibilities diminish.

Twenty minutes pass. The dogs lose interest.
The violent, imagined world recedes.
I return to bed, rediscover
the warmth of my lover's body
beneath the covers. I want to tell her
I understand our mind's need to know
its limits. How far will the world bend
in the dark night before we scream? Or sing?

Tall Trees

This is the place of tall trees,
trees that walk at night.
Spreading their roots
over the earth's surface,
they hold the soul of the world
in their embrace.
Do not be afraid. They know
they are the flesh of our flesh.
When fierce winds blow out of valleys,
they bend to kiss our eyes. Caressing
shadows, they are gentle creatures.
In love with the indigo sky,
they imagine us with our hands in the air.
They forgive us the pain we bring
with our fear of unknown shapes.
Between sunrise and sundown,
they stand breathless, and move
only when the wind breathes their name.

Cathedral Grove

Rime of a winter's
day freezes
words upon your lips

Kneel, at last,
in the dark arches
of this word-shaped
cathedral
       The sun,
from behind ice-topped
trees
     blinds you
Cup the light
in your palms

form it into
the perfect image
of prayer

Insomnia

Sleeping is something I should have learned
how to do after fifty years of practice.
Often I lie awake at night
planning strategies for getting to sleep.
Once I've drifted off, I can't remember
how I did it.
                    In the morning, a gleam of light
outlines the mountains, rises into the blue sky,
and like a siren swoops down across the strait.
Exposed to its full glare, I am seduced
by the blinding brightness of a midday summer sun;
but like sails luffing in a sea breeze,
vague recollections stir at night
and the problem of sleep arises again.

New tricks need to be invented — a
language of sleep. I dream of places
where memory is stone and the breath
of busy streets touches my slumbering face.
With my fingers, I draw maps in the earth
and people unburdened with history
rejoice when they learn the art of song.

Sometimes, when my lover is asleep, I
imagine a beautiful woman
whose emptiness will only be filled
by my affections.

I love to get lost with the reassurance
of a map to guide me. I define sleep
as a lexicographer would: a black hole
into which the soul falls; the breathless
terror of oblivion; loss of awareness;
a petal folding; dormancy; a road
travelled alone towards our beginnings;

with upon, *denoting postponement*
of a decision till the following day, 1519
(the *OED's* precision is admirable); *with* in,
to sleep on the premises where one
is employed; with off, *to get rid of, 1552;*
idle; like a log; counting sheep.

Because we live on an island
we believe there is an edge
to our universe
and sleep is where we settle
beyond the wake of high tide
and the urge to slip into the sea.

Suddenly I sit up and laugh. Everyone
is lost in their own dream of God.
I see them on beds of lotus petals
and realize sleep is where I am not.

I look at the woman lying beside me,
watch the rapid movement of her green eyes,
wonder who is she, where has she flown to?

I imagine her naked, off in some distant place.
I want to touch her, she is so near, but
I fear I might startle her and she will awake
to another name, in another room.

About me the house is alive. I listen
to the groaning and moaning of wood,
the rumble of pipes and ducts, wind blowing
through the sashes of northfacing windows.
I rise, move from room to room, brush against
ghosts, those who speak from behind their tears —
they too, would once more see their faces.

No birdsongs, voices, traffic noises
interrupt the breathing of the dusty house.
This is when I understand with certainty
I can speak to myself, curious to know
where in this dark world I am.

Words Compose You

Words compose you, words as rare
and beautiful as the Sanskrit
songs you speak softly from beyond
this wall that separates us. *Maya*,
you whisper. Truth that devours
flesh. Communion before the light.
What spells you cast. What forbidden
image slips through your hands and falls
to the floor to be swept
away and tossed into the fire
of invisible completions?
Does the scent of spices rise
in the flames? How quickly passions fade
in absence. Agni, god of fire
and transformation, I see
smoke climbing to the heavens. Toward
the mutable clarity of form.
A dry moon shines in a dark sky.
What might we say: that we are beloved
when we know that to speak is divine.

When Do We Begin

When do we begin to understand
these moments are never more
than what is forgotten;
that each second
held in your arms
leaves me out of breath —
with one less heartbeat.

If only we could forget
the lies of a thousand summers,
forget photographs
detached
from who we have become . . .

and remember instead
the beauty of plum blossoms
scattered in the ancient dance
of acrobatic winds;
remember instead
the fanfare of cut flowers
arranged in a vase —
an interlude in sunlight.

The trick is to accept
what we have imagined.
Perhaps it is time to give up poetry
for the sake of the garden;
plants are so forgiving.

We watch
the gambolling flight of butterflies,
their yellow wings frayed,
drawn to the exotic buddleia.

This afternoon we walk together
along a brick path
laid with our own calloused hands.

Here is no monument.

We are bound by worn edges
and the memory of a way
we have travelled before.

Where is the Memory

Where is the memory
that holds us captive
in the night? In dreams
that bring sweat to the sheets
or bring the knit of secrecy
to eyes that move rapidly
before the naked figure
of an unexpected love?

She clutches roses to her breasts
and smiles at the small wounds
opening into her skin. She forgives.

Should I weep for our dying
or embrace the woman
who mocks my solitude?
Those who look at my eyes alone
will think I sleep. Will say
I fight the weight of stones.
These are such dead days.

Should I desire to kiss her
even though I grow old
and the light of stars
deserts the vacant sky?

Notebook from the Garden

Without complaint, my wife
lifts her back against the earth —

happy to see a lump of dark soil
break against the tines of her fork.

Small enough, the garden
accommodates her labour.

Her shadow, busy still
forgives me

who watches idle in sunlight.

What the Poet Sees

Last week you cut your hair short,
a freshness, you said; to see yourself
differently; to angle a new image
at the world. A manly cut,
you laughed, and then confessed
you had grown tired of being
the tall blonde with shoulder-length hair,
always brushing aside heads
turned to glance at you from crown to toe.
You waved a kerchief in the air —
(A truce? I wondered.)
In the past week, you mused, not one man's
looked in my direction.

Desire's Equation

What must we think
when fear
amplifies this grey world

and birds arc across the sky
their song
the sonic boom of flight
into silence.

Desire's equation.

Night's black ink
seeps into spaces
between branches of maple
alder and hawthorne. Winter
is upon us, love's arms empty
except for the air
stirred
by the perpetual
movement of wings.

So, our thoughts migrate
towards the sun
and flowering honeysuckle
the ceremony of birdsong
the birth of trembling leaves

the sound and motion of absence:
our longing.

The Light That Dwells in Names

And do you believe in God, after all?
Well, there are those moments,
foreboding in the memories they bring,
when everything seems hopeless,
beyond my powers, and, yes, I kneel
and pray for a little extra help.
I try to imagine someone like Wagner
perched on a precipice of doubt.
I don't know about the other business,
heaven, an after-life, but there are times
when solitude settles on the cold edges
of the world and leaves me so alone
I seek another heart racing. My lips quiver
as I awaken to cry for help. My eyes
feel the burden of shame and consequence.
How I crave the joy of a hand
reaching out of the earth for mine
and squeezing hard, extending the assurance
that comes with a wink or that lingers
in still air like the scent of a lily.

Evangelical

So many theories abound
each a decoy to chaos
and I wonder if the universe
expands at the same rate
as souls enter the heavens.

What a crowd will gather
when all the dream worlds collide
and all the choruses, speeches,
lyrics, cheers, and weeping implode.
What a bang!
Such energy, such big talk!

Then, those who preach the end
will never know
how we gain momentum
and glory from their words;
how they accelerate us on tongues of fire
as we spin ever further
into space, red shifting to infinity.

Eyes Through Which We Travel

We do not speak the same language, yet
she comes to me, her hands stirring the air,
her eyes quick as a cat's. My Greek guest
would like to know what lies beyond
her sight, concealed from her by distance.
She points to the mountains across the strait,
the islands, the gulls swarming after herring,
a windsurfer riding a two-foot chop.
I loan her my telescope and wonder,
how differently do we see the world?
What shade of blue colours her sky? What shade
of green the sea? Does she see the heron
whose choreographed stride through the shallows
has all the grace of a Grecian benediction?
Here there are no porticos, temples or olive trees,
no myrtle, or cicadas thrumming in the seagrass.
I want her to see the imperceptible air, to linger
where the wilderness has become the most recent ruin.
Words tumble over words. She stands
and flings her arms out as if embracing
a colossus, and then pulls her hands
toward her breasts, folds her arms
and holds herself. She turns, looks
into my eyes and sees I am puzzled
by her joy. Through her daughter she says,
"You can't imagine how close I am!"

Inside the Eye

Inside the eye, cones
gifted with the shape
of pines, fragrance
reminiscent of light
travelling swifter than
the spell of memory.

We embrace sight
and so through the eye,
song searches for the throat,
sings praise for the sun
cradled in an emerald sky.

Risking the Light

Before us, a pinpoint in space
so radiant, angels open their wings
to shield their eyes from knowing
an agony beyond flesh.

Beyond the wounded hand of God,
we discover an equation
in a slight turn of leaves
towards the sun —

pages released from
escapable darkness.

At the Centre of the Dark

for James Baldwin

Moon, you rode the night over angel acres
eclipsed by earth, a halo rising
through clouds that mark these boundaries in time;
cast aside trees and sea, the living air.

I read the root inside these words
and start to dream of ancestors;
struggle to be reborn, await the light
reflection of the sun marauding the skies.

Listen: the heavens balance uneasily
between hydrogen, helium and carbon;
between the first voice and silence; between
prophecy and the ghosts who call this home.

The Radiant Gift

Thousands of starlings occupy the trees
outside her bedroom window. Theirs
is the mad chatter of multitudes.
She begins to count them, but they fly
from fir to cedar, from cedar to hemlock.
They show no preference in their celestial ways.
They swoop down, suicidal divers, to feed
on the berries of pyracantha, and dart
back into their open space. They know
their place outside catechism. Birds
in this season of snow accept
the radiant gift. Delicate white flowers
surrounded by thorns, turned in autumn
to poisonous red, their crown and flesh inflamed.

In her dreams, nothing remains bodiless,
not even this perfect denial of desire and love;
not even her slumbering image of Christ
borne into the sky on the wings of birds.

Looking East

I'm getting nowhere fast,
I loudly complain.

Progress at last,
whispers the Buddha.

The Fourth Moon of Broadway

This is the avenue I remember, straight and wide.
This is the city of trees at night, fired
from the belly busting rage and swagger that chain
brother to brother. This is the city that dwells
in the tribal power of invincible youth, the will
to walk the streets in the glow of making history
from hunger and blood, the blood of prisoner and lover alike.
I wait for those who watch the slanting rain
and seek the flesh of new bone, flowers bursting into the sky
out of the appetite of skeletons, the orange blooms of night
shucked from the fourth moon of Broadway, melons
glowing overhead in the nightmare chambers
of storefronts. This is not Damascus, though dusk burns
everlasting in the recitation of the names of our beloved.
This is the will of the deal; to host the flesh reborn
from solitude, to linger at the height of orgasm.
This is the gift I hold in moonlight, soft
and transparent, open to what the heart and body crave.
This is the avenue I remember, straight and wide.

Partners

Referendum Day, October 26, 1992

Two men fighting in the street begin
from habit — confirm the invisible.
The same brown bag rests against the wall
where each has pissed away his emptiness;

where each has reconstructed history,
built stories from razed and burning towns.
Spinning and shuffling in the winter rain,
they return to the feeble dance that swirls

in their brains; to a madcap exchange of vows
where yesterday will always be absent.
They are partners who swing at each other;
lovers whose lips cut on the end of a fist.

Each desires to speak of love but that word
lives in a remote and separate moment of their lives,
when each in search of the soul of tenements
was promised a long, long life and easy money.

One convulses at the thought, draws a knife,
a new twist added by the tilting scale of night.
The blade rips into the other's belly,
a deep wound. When did they begin to feud?

Their private war scatters pigeons into
an asphalt sky. Winter lurks behind their eyes
and the torn man feels the cold push up
into his heart. This country is muted.

The man with the knife in his hand steps aside,
stares at the figure lying in the street —
the scene before him is another story;
the corpse belongs to someone else's indignation.

Smoke from an alley fire chokes his cries
and he flings his arms and body back
against the wall and fears to close his eyes
on the one who has abandoned him.

Fires of Chernobyl

I

April 26, 1986

As we watch the news, my son and I see
you plunge into the blaze. We are puzzled

by the spade you hold in your hands. Who are you?
A blood-red sun explodes in the tortured sky.

The house of cards that carries you to your death
is falling down. Say it will die with you.

Say that the graphite debris you shovel
down into the sarcophagus feeds

the political will; that the State
leaves you to your solitude, to enjoy

the last threads of light before you are collected
into darkness, into a forest of crosses.

Say others care as I do for your sacrifice.
Say your act is embedded in our minds

as is our love for rivers, clear air and growing things.
Say that in going into the inferno, into the dead zone

invisible as it is, you have healed my mind
and closed the wound. As I turn the dark earth,

I will sing for you. My garden is green
and my voice strong. When your body is taken

and laid in the ground, may your spirit live here
and others find it green and growing and abundant.

May your children feel at home in our place.
May they know that wherever they go in their dreams

they walk on their father's ashes, with their father's
love. May they know they walk on sacred ground.

II

1991, The Globe and Mail

Dr. Chernousenko, physicist, reveals
officials ordered him to "liquidate the consequences."

This is the power of murderers. The magic
to turn light into darkness, energy to mass:

to reverse equations, invite apocalypse.
To set men on fire, blind to what they would destroy.

My son says he finally understands. He can see
through the wall of words. He can feel the torment

of the men who danced the minute waltz
on the rooftop, their eyes extinguished like coals,

their dragons never to be slain by the sword.
For thirty kilometres, the country they love is haunted

by the ghosts of fields and forests and villages.
35 million people damaged, Mr. Chernousenko says.

Beyond boundaries, death rides the winds and a child
traces shapes of imaginary beasts in faraway clouds.

Things As They Are

A full moon, suffering, things as they are.
From our room we can hear the world's wounded
In the cries of children who will never know
The blue electric fires of midnight, the surge
Of light that burns in their intricate bodies.
Naked ghosts, what are we to believe?
Words choke in the mouths of prophets —
Under a sheltering sky, the silent, breathless air.

To be with you at this moment
When those who go mad in the summer heat
Speak from behind homicidal masks
Is to listen to the words of the disinherited.
To watch with you while mothers sit, cross-legged,
In swirling dust on the stoops of huts
Or weep in doorways that open onto
The dried blood of murderous streets —

Is to need to embrace you in this distant room.
As we seek the unspoken name of God,
The recurring filaments of memory
Flash, like moths, in the conjuring light.
Vacant future, power lies only in the ability
To draw a breath. Harmony, you say, is sleep
Settling on wide eyes without the fear of death —
When the spirit no longer begs, *kill me*!

To be with you when this luminous haze
Resounds with rumours of carrion birds,
Is to know the mystery that saves us in love.
Circling through this long day of betrayals
Confirms we are wise to be wary
Of the world. A full moon in a dark sky
Astonishes us with the weight of predictions.
Why does the sun linger so indulgently over the dead?

Reflections burn a path of embers
Across the sea. Candles ignite the stars.
Tonight the moon is in perigee, as close
To earth as it has been in twenty-five years.
Tonight we see the world's plagues
Through the eyes of others. Shadows
Weep across this room and bind us —
Witness to their cold and lighted passage.

2
_____

Seasonal

To speak quietly at such a distance, to speak
And to be heard is to be large in space,
That, like your own, is large, hence, to be part
Of sky, of sea, large earth, large air. It is
To perceive men without reference to their form.

— Wallace Stevens

NICOLE: *January 6*

This epiphany, minus Media and Persia,
minus the Magi, ancient names and myths gone old.
We live out our lives behind these shadows,
come to know each other so briefly
crossing beneath the dead light of this winter's moon.
Only this sound, mystery of flight,
night birds landing on the waters of Nanoose Bay,
the surf scoters and buffleheads.

"I go round and round," you say, "become dizzy
when I think of the world turning."
Your stopped voice hangs in the cold air.
Somewhere near, moonlight washes up to stone,
marks this path along the shore;
our hands, frozen voices, held in communion.

NICOLE: *February 24*

Snowbells, the first flower's unfolding, mimed
in your own small hands. You exclaim: "But they
didn't pop their showing yet," and you glance at me,
quizzical, your hands opening to the February sky.
Last night, you talked out in your sleep
while I, in the next room, had pale dreams
of graveyards and tombstones, beyond
which no language can invent, wrote my own
epitaph, a consuming indulgence. And you, you
too, closing into your own darkness, asked
the hall light be left on, confident to see yourself to sleep.
Today, though I fear I might not see
your words form images, shaped by the hand in gesture,
we are astonished by snowbells impelled toward sunlight.

NICOLE: *March 20*

Spring equinox, the day's own turning, declines
into a dance of dust, into stone. From tidal pools
small pincers claw toward you, your own face
half lighted by the sun's descent, a small moon
caught in the spring's first light. In the telescope
you sight the moons of Jupiter, and I
push to explain gravity, tides, that planets are spheres
suspended in this dusk, in orbit around the sun,
that where we stand, on the edge of this sea,
half circled by the bay, is also a planet.
Puzzled, you reply, "I know all I know; each night
the moon comes down to my room to play with me."
Stones, I rush upon you as shore crabs scurry
before the turn of tides, and the heart's bleeding.

NICOLE: *April 3*

"It is storming. There is lightning.
Clouds are crashing down on to the roofs.
The people are running out."

Do your people, like mine, run about in circles,
their hearts snared by nightmare fire,
white of the lily consumed in flame?

I wish you more than scarred dreams, bloodied hands
holding the compass of masked apologies,
eyes of vacant stone violating our silence:

Peace is no guarantee against war.
Hell's music outrages the dead;
no prayer but this requiem rising from ash.

Magnolia and cherry blossoms bloom,
the terrestrial storms outside our home.

NICOLE: May 11

Was it the day of the whale, a large grey
drawn to unfamiliar shores?

Was it the night you spoke in tongues, mutable
archaeology of the moon's betrayal?

"They were scared behind my eyes.
They came out of my dreams."

Do not lament the loss of giant bones;
we cannot know the shape of time.

Nor can I offer you another's history,
only my longing to share in this, these words.

We come to these islands as if to dream,
come to trees where we ascend to their growing.

We come to these islands as if to mystery,
come to a sea where voice is song.

NICOLE: *June 21*

Since last we measured your height against the doorjamb
you have grown precisely three and half inches.
You are more than pleased with summer's whirling play.
"Was it crows who swallowed the moon?"
"Why do stars light up at night?" Such questions
tempt me to turn somersaults; stand me on my head.
Doors to our fears open with equations
more complex than the random geometry
of celestial configurations. Now we wheel
around the world at arm's length, your laughter
muted as your feet swing round, circle above the lawn.
Wearied of this flight, I spin you gently down.
At once you leap lightly into my arms and laugh:
"Look, I tricked gravity! That's what pulls you down!"

NICOLE: *July 28*

Madrona, arbutus, demonic tree
sheds leaves and bark through summer;
the scent of October ripens the air.
Childhood you cannot abandon so easily.
You navigate the seasons, as if dancing
at the helm of things were heaven's will.
The way of stone encircles our hearts.

We open our eyes to the music of memory,
legends sung by wind; songs composed in our throats.
You took your first steps as if they recorded
your name in the radiant moments of morning.
Now you rush toward me, your delicate mouth
filled with apple; as we embrace
you laugh and sing: "There, that's an apple kiss."

NICOLE: *August 20*

In summer the sun ascends from the sea,
a silent verb of morning, and the song of birds
sits on your tongue: "Why is tomorrow, tomorrow?"
Or, "When I grow up, do you grow down?"
Such a knot of questions would have defeated
even Alexander. Five years ago, to the day
what a blessing was born under that fragile moon.

Daughter, in love we betray what we know
by default — bloom of the rose is holy.
Now balloons, streamers, cake and candles
decorate the playroom. "Roses," you say
"I love them, I can smell them with my heart."
If I were an old man would I answer
only a fool comes to age with ease?

NICOLE: *September 3*

Tonight, driving home, headlamps prying the darkness
you question me about the birth of your brother.
Above, beyond the skeletal twists of arbutus,
a bright star follows us through the motions,
turns in the highway, my responses now
as oblique as the moonlit forms
plunging at us from the forest's verge.
You cannot know what I have known, at best, imperfectly.
Nearing home, I seek an easy solution and tell you
when you are old enough, you'll understand — these
noble illusions of fleshless bone. "No," you cry. "Why
can't I stay five? I don't want to die!" And your fingers
close, like calipers around mine, measure this moment
against his birth: close us in a matrix of shadow, of flesh.

NICOLE: October 31

Bats and hobgoblins fly about the house.
You search for the seeds from our last fall
harvest of pumpkins and plant them in a jar
to watch them sprout. You ask your mother
"What happens after death?" Next morning
you announce: "I believe those who say
we are reborn. They are right! I'll never
pull the legs from crabs again. They might be me!"
What we know, we live by.
This mutilation of night, eve of All Saints' Day
smiling behind toothless grins of candlelight,
terrifies me. You grow so quickly
toward us. There is nothing difficult
in simple questions. The seed grows its own.

NICOLE: *November 11*

Things not past remembrance: daughter, first born,
how your brother clings to his mother,
his sightless eyes open, suspicious.

His small body lurches about against her belly
risking the perils of uncharted voyage,
desperate to recall those inner waters;

as if barnacles latched onto rock
distrusting the rush of tides,
small lives parented by the sea.

Daughter, love inspires your desire to birth,
to eclipse his life. Without malice, the tide
takes measure of its own motions.

Abandoned on shore, fathers listen,
hear the insistent weeping of mothers.

NICOLE: *December 24*

How to tell you your brother's birth
brings more than mere recurrence. More than
a sky host of shore birds, heron and gulls,
returning to this bay, drawn to the known
currents of habit, the easy feed
of herring and shellfish. "My dreams hide
behind my eyes, only come out when I speak them."

To name what we know, to hear the space
between words is to welcome strangers
into our house and hearts. How readily
we discard this old magic, these animals
spun from the trees, that leap from fires;
those shadow beings etched into wind
where gull wings lift our voices into air.

OWEN: *June 28*

You stand beneath the hoop, ball in hand
all forty-two inches poised on feet smaller than
Kareem's, Magic's or Bird's big toe, and you look up
past the backboard, ten feet to the heavens beyond,
bend down, launch the ball skyward, miss again
and again until, swish through the net, twenty-three
times that first day. What does Piaget know?
How you circle and guard against our expectations.

Listen, forget that you are only four.
Forget that you actually sunk the ball.
Tell me, are we too bold with advice, our dreams
accidentally prompting revenge, Hamlet cast in tennis shoes?
This morning your mother greeted you with "Howdy sunshine!"
And you, quick to rebound, replied: "Morning raincloud."

OWEN: *September 2*

When I'm sixteen, you say, I'll be over
six feet tall and I'll slam dunk you with a move
along the base line. As graceful as Michael Jordan
I'll take to the air, my arms stretched to full height,
your body held aloft, gliding slow-motion through time
towards the hoop and net, your eyes bugging
out of their sockets.
                    Together we'll climb the stars.

This is personal. This is how you measure yourself
against your father — to pivot on our love,
wheel and soar into the future, burning
to know who you are. I want to ask:
How can you be so certain you'll please me?
Or is this a pilgrimage we all make
blind with the credulity of a beggar?

OWEN: *December 22*

To speak of love in this season is to speak
through the distance of cold nights, of sons born
remembering names spoken from the bloodied
lips of dark nations. In this silence of earth
simple truths reside unfurrowed. You say, "We were
born in different ways. Nicole and me
were born from you and dad. You guys were born
from the Indians, since they were here first."

So, stories start, live their lives out and die
inside each of us; yet, every man begs
to know the winter rose, the fragile stem
thrust from the frozen earth. Invisible sons
help us to recall the future, reborn
in the roots of familiar voices.

3

Enchantment
& Other Demons

Enchantment & Other Demons

As the woman approaches him in his garden, he recalls the line, breathe deeply the gathering gloom. Darkness swirls around his feet. He is certain that if he pays this woman the slightest attention she will be annoyed. Yet a sense of vanity and erotic melancholy pushes him to the edge of humiliation.

Insane. He has never met this person before. Admittedly, she has a presence. Something which makes him feel effaced. A dread he can only explain as a lack of sunlight.

He wants to leaf curl in on himself, find a disguise, as the conductor of an orchestra or as a foot soldier; as a blossom on a Yoshina cherry or as a frog in a pond. He longs to erase any resemblance he might have to the original words and blood of memory. He can feel a root in his mind tear, a sure signal that an invasion has occurred. There is a breach in his defences.

Her entrance is quick and thorough. He senses the ground slipping under his feet. Trees speed by, fast forward.

She says she's a stockbrocker. That she's in a hurry. She wishes to know everything he knows about gardens, about the virtues of mulch.

Her shoulder-length, auburn hair flies out from side to side, a counter balance to her bouncing stride. She tells him people in the village have described and praised his gardens. He is portrayed as an arboreal Monet, although no one has ever noticed him, brush in hand, standing dreamily before a canvas. Her lips part, seductively he thinks, and a chuckle escapes between her white teeth.

He attempts to explain to her that he is just completing construction on a meditation garden. He has not built it as a place in which to meditate but rather for what it might reveal to him about the nature of meditation. A spring breeze blows against his face. Why does he feel as if he is flirting with a scorpion whose tail will catch him in the confusion of his own hypnotic trance?

With a sweep of her hand she dismisses the clean, spare look of his new creation, plants isolated, alone, in their own patch of ground. Too much the sense of a still life, she concludes. She prefers the cluttered look, the fullness of an English country garden replete with vegetables and fruit trees, hedges and rose beds. Vegetation ordered but blended, balanced and manicured. A garden in full bloom.

He is perplexed. Has he not just told her that where they stand is at the centre of a new world? That the mulch will blend with the existing soil and the plants grow into each other over the seasons? Form released into infinite shapes through time.

She surveys his work, not with pleasure, but with politeness. As she turns, she points to an area beneath two towering Douglas firs. Appearances are the key here, she says. A garden is best when it can be left untended. Or, better still, abandoned. And it will still produce. Like a healthy stock. Bluechip. Secure. With a high interest yield.

Inadvertently he is caught up in her enthusiasm and flair for enterprise. Briefly he feels aroused, a burning in his groin. Tears come to his eyes. He is shocked to realize that although they speak the same language, the words have different meanings. This realization increases his need to speak.

He bends forward and carefully prunes the candles on a Tanyosho pine.

Some things can't be rushed, he says, although he feels embarrassed by his spells of desire. He remembers what Francis Quarles said: "A fool's heart is in his tongue; but a wise man's tongue is in his heart."

He lifts a branch of full-grown Pieris to expose the delicate white horn of a Trillium. Take at least a year to know your garden, he continues, and then, even then, consider what you have beheld, what small fragment of the universe the shutter of your eye has glimpsed. For in the next moment, if night and dream have a place at all in our lives, you will feel the chill of recollection and know there was a time, a time when the order of the world called us beloved.

The woman turns and speaks back over her shoulder. You've lived too long in the shadow of your plants and trees. You're beginning to grow moldy. Where's the profit in that?

He smiles, for he knows he will be here long after she has departed. He imagines she will ride the wind at the speed of light.

He wriggles his toes in the moss and feels the earth embrace his feet.

The Angler/Poet: Parable of a Sporting Life

In and out of the shadows, we follow the path that follows the river. An old friend, who claims to be both poet and angler, tells me he doesn't like sport fishing, that returning a fish to water with the memory of a hook in its mouth is a perversion spawned by the tyranny of guilt. You must prefer murder, I say. No, he replies, some species were meant to be hunted, others to be hunters — that's obvious. As the man who survives his execution never forgets the feel of the rope around his neck, so too the fish never forgets the hook in its mouth. Or the poet the memory of the line that escapes late at night on the edges of sleep.

But the analogy is false, I argue. The man who escapes his execution also avoids the final surrender — when the soul stands on the edge of transmutation.

At a bend in the river, in the deep green glass that pools beneath the alders, a large steelhead noses between smooth river stones.

Yes, he agrees, or to borrow from the parlance of fishing, the one that got away. What wonderful fables conspire in our collaborations.

We delight in the prospect of setting our hooks into Milton's Leviathan:

> *Hugest of living creatures, on the deep*
> *Stretch'd like a promontory, sleeps or swims,*
> *And seems a moving land, and at his gills*
> *Draws in, and at his trunk spouts out a flood.*

Such are the fish of our deepest dreams. Ahab's Moby. The Old Man and his giant Marlin. Holy Abtu and Anet.

My friend baits his hook, flicks his wrist and we both listen to the melodic whirl of the reel.

We want this creature to come to death with grace and dignity, he says. But who initiates the terrifying death dance? Us or him? We fear, as much as he does, to look down the long tunnel toward the vision in the mirror, distorted and faded. What tempest grows within us as the kill rises in our throat? No flag of truce waves before the battle.

The fisherman and poet long to control the crescent moon that sinks into the sea as the September sun rises into a new season.

We angle after the dance of return, he says.

With a sudden flick of its tail, the steelhead shatters the surface, shards of water spraying into the stillness of air. A gaping mouth swallows the fly.

We desire to run our hands over its silver skin, the chain metal, polished, that peels away the water as it dodges our masquerade. At dusk we listen to the stories of men who have returned from journeys, and who repeat the songs of memory — the cold descent into the eyes of gulls and eagles, cormorants and herons.

Time passes against the pull of the line. We discuss preparations for the feast. The poet, he says, should always celebrate his catch.

Feathering to Infinity

for David Phillips and Hugh Proctor

When the carpenter set his square into corners and took measurements from the recently bared studs and joists, he found the floor in our home bowed and warped in every direction. Nothing was level or straight. The entrance hall sloped at least four inches to the south and had been built in a different season, on a day when rainfall transcended indifference. I can feather the floor out to infinity, he said, and he began to cut pieces of plywood, shaped into huge wedges of pearled pine, and placed one on top of another to raise one corner to the level of the others. He took a reading from his compass, tapped the barometer, and moved slowly outward, toward the horizon. As he grew smaller and we feared he'd reach infinity, we told him he'd best return. You're one heart beat from vertical, we yelled, from where the lark's song spills into nightfall. We'll learn to live with the slope in the floor, I pleaded. Bow, my wife corrected. We'll learn to adapt, I said. We'll learn to walk with one leg shorter than the other, she said. Better that than lose a fine artisan, not to mention a friend, she added.

On the last day we saw him, he was a speck on the earth's cusp, our floor as flat as an oak table top, a slice of marble, or a ploughed field hiding naked under a prairie sky.

Neither of us has remarked on the incline in years, nor can we recall how it was before. Before the spiders left the comfort of their nests. Before their cobwebs were torn and the sun broke through windows as if through the spokes of a wheel. Each spring, we quarrel about which corner the potted fern slipped in to before our world became perfectly flat. But the carpenter is more than a memory, for it was he who brought proportion into our lives and made us see the beauty of figures and words woven in the wrist.

Naming the Song

for Bob K.

Our wish for you, my friend, is to be forever in fine
voice, for you have sung gentle, ferocious, sad, drunken,
bawdy, naked, clothed, dreaming, cheating, lying,
evasive, pop, postmodern, tender, horny, occasional —
this ordering is discreet and with purpose — testy,
listing, wayward, seedy, sketchy, erotic, romantic,
loathing, raucous, crowing, longing (need I go on),
silent songs (such a list might include tunes, hymns,
chants) at the prairie sky;

songs with fists, that strike at that flatland wind;

songs with faces, that colour orange the way of the
sun;

songs with flesh, that taste of the faint light of lemons
picked at dawn;

songs with feet, that dance in the fading steps of buffalo;

songs with tears, that dwell nameless in the nether
regions of onions;

songs with heart, that long to mend the constancy of
separation;

songs with eyes, that follow home the flight of crows and magpies;

songs with genitals, that seed the garden with the sorrow of absence;

songs with lips, that kiss the bones sleeping below the river run;

songs with breath, that whisper the echoing of a stonehammer's ring and know the ways of ancestors;

songs with legs, that wrap around and cradle an ecstasy you could not define (a magical island in a Greek sea or the Garden of Harmony in Old Age);

songs with nipples, that desire the language of eyes and mouths, that mirror the moon and tides;

songs with hands, that trace the fragments of letters from an unknown Semitic alphabet (did you imagine you were making love with Astarte?);

songs with tongues, that seek the rim of the sky and freeze on the metal of winter;

songs with assholes (are there limits to the artistic application of body parts?);

songs with memories, that pursue dreams over the edges of time into a hotel room inhabited by drunks, lovers, explorers, morticians, farmers, (is it fair to include the ten fulsome ladies from the Carlton Highland in Edinburgh?), politicians, hockey players, professors, wives (lest we forget), fools, horsemen, Indians, printers, poets, demons, tricksters and whores (not necessarily in that order):

my friend, Empedocles discovered the invisible air; you, in turn, fill our mouths with words and waggle our tongues with the world's invisible songs.

The Lost Sister

. . . appearances and words speak so differently; the visual
never allows itself to be translated intact into the verbal.
                    —John Berger

In time they spoke of her as the lost sister.

෧

Seven beautiful sisters, the Pleiades, daughters of Atlas,
are pursued by Orion. Fearing the violent nature of
the giant hunter, the sisters pray to the gods to change
their forms. Taking pity on them, Jupiter turns them
into pigeons and then gives them a place as a group of
stars in the constellation of Taurus. The seventh sister,
not wanting to witness the ruin of Troy, the city so
lovingly built by her son, flees the sky. Her six sisters,
shocked by the horrible sight they witnessed, have
looked pale ever since.

෧

This is how it came to pass that her heart beats in an
imageless universe. How to reach her, to hold a shadow
that walks the depths of an early morning sky, imagined
in the smooth and rapturous rising of the sun.

෧

Her memory whirls through a chaos of images, a dreamscape of confusing and puzzling dimensions. She sinks into a free-fall dream and it is all she can do to pull herself back up again. Her brain is on fire.

ã

When she was younger she dreamt of parallel dimensions. What a person did at any moment in their lives determined their fate. The same was true for story. Once the first line had been written, the tale was as much as told. Variations abounded, but the essence was the same. For instance, she could never escape the memory of walking in the fields outside the small coastal town in which she had grown up. There, amongst the flowers, she would dwell in the privacy of her own dreams.

Her mind glided into a field of flowers. Lilies and violets, columbine and asphodel. She dreamt of a land covered in dew. Slowly the night air warmed into morning. During the day she sucked the sunlight from the stems of nasturtium. As the sky bled into orange, the memory of the fabulous dance of northern lights flashed in her eyes. The mysteries of nature comforted her, but the mystery of her own disappearance was a frightening deception. Even her own senses betrayed her.

ã

What she cannot discover is the thread that links where she is and what has happened to her; what she can tell anyone willing to listen is that time and space are subjective and capricious concepts at best. Her place in time seems arbitrary. She could as easily be Joan of Arc or Anne Boleyn, Titania or Viola. And space, space is a shadow game. Whoever is under the lights has the stage. Does this mean the audience exists elsewhere?

ॐ

Another useless speculation which slides into her mind, sideways, out of the blue. Her brain appears to have developed the habit of recollecting the nonessential. She can call up insignificant details from cold storage but the slightest hint of revelation or tidbit of gossip that might explain what has happened to her remains buried in darkness. Exhaustion. She is the victim of one long breathless silence. Or perhaps she has been abducted by creatures of fire. The Jinn. This is silly. An illusion.

ॐ

Intuition. She senses that she has encountered the vilest creatures to crawl out of the sewers of the world. The fire at the belly's centre.

ॐ

This bizarre explanation of what has happened to her comes clouded and wrapped in ages of memory. Through all the women she has been, she hears her mother's voice calling. The heavy flow of waters. Rivers spanning centuries. The fall behind the eyes into the caverns of the dead.

Always, always a dream of gardens. The forbidden fruit. The food of binding. Indenture. A dream of elves. Of little men with giant bellies. Of women screaming out of the whites of their eyes.

⁊₰

She praises and envies all those women who are blessed with multiple personalities, for they can love, hate, regret, weep, laugh, and, above all else, dream. They're not prisoners of their own boredom and loss. They're free of gravity, and all the lesser laws of nature.

Absurd. She is digressing. She must escape whatever dimension, time and space, she occupies. The devil, the underworld, theology, reason — these are the constructs of man. She longs to embrace Artemis or Sappho, to be free.

She wants to be brave. She wants to look the devil square in the eye. Her heart will break into a million pieces — stars enough to fill the heavens — her six sisters weak in the glare of multitudes.

She must escape. She is the lost sister.

4

Arabesque

Now is the time of the Assassins.
        — Rimbaud

Eternity is hardly longer than life.
        — Char

If the union of two lovers comes about through love, it involves the idea of death, murder or suicide. This aura of death is what denotes passion . . . only in the violation, through death if need be, of the individual's solitariness can there appear that image of the beloved object which in the lover's eyes invests all being with significance.
        — Bataille

White, white, white, but it is summer and hot, snow is in the mind. White walls, white sheets, white bodies, white paper. Forms glimmer. Apparitions stalk the streets of this near white concrete mirage of a city. Home from an early evening at the beach, our minds littered with paper wrappers, empty bottles and excited children playing in the sand and sea. Large shapes appear in the sky, their powerful wings white shadows over the mountains. The sun sets, faces dissolve, sightless mannequins adrift on the window glass. Outside, silhouettes drift by, targets in a shooting gallery, stagey ghosts dancing through dusk before disappearing into darkness.

ع

We wish on the first star, the mad hatter — you are the mad hatter — and I. Together, naked between white sheets, our dreams play variations on similar correspondences, on the arabesque of forms. Cool thoughts reject the hot dusty sand of the beach for white walls, white sheets and snow. We touch and our thoughts swim in the flow of our bodies.

Lying on the wool rug we bought in North Africa, we dream, a town in the north, a small log cabin. We lounge, warmed before a fire. All the wealth of Croesus. One shutter bangs freely against the outside wall; snow paints itself on the window panes. The door is bolted by a heavy wooden crosspiece, but still . . . hinges squeak in the wind. Outside, hunters stalk these woods for game, rearrange this dream. Pit-lamping, death dance of light. Besides the flicker of the fire, a candle casts a halo on the ceiling. A painting, a moon slipping through the fold of a cloud, the edges lighting the inner circles of the gods. In a corner, on a table, stands a Buddha named Baudelaire. A reflection in the mirror on the wall behind . . .

ð

Blessed be all of you, angels of snow.

We rise when its late and the night air cools our kitchen above the front stairs of the apartment house where we live. A cheap bottle of red, red wine stands on the table. A late supper, a chess board, a thirst. In this devils heat of a dying summer sun our bodies perspire. The night is as quiet as bones. Only the fragrance of roses and the scent of sea wrack wafts on the air.

You push a white pawn to a black square, and wine, sipping wine. A black pawn to a white square, a late supper of cheese, biscuits and wine. You move too fast, downing wine and your body twists. You move too fast and your bellys hollow.

&

O people, I am ready to invent love and laughter if only you will plant the nocturnal rose. It will taste of wine.

I stand on a square large enough to hold my six foot frame. Impatiently, I push my pawns forward, a novice at this game. As several men converge on the same square I realize I must sacrifice at least one piece, and later, many of them. I begin to sweat, to feel the heat, the pressure of the narrowly formed corridors and square shaped slabs. Like hungry gods, we manipulate our pawns in this mock battle. We are serious in this game.

A voice cries out, my voice, from beyond shadows, beyond death. Too often we cast love after barren hearts. So our words arrive in silence.

You recline on the sofa, press wine to your lips. I am first to lose a man. Your hand waves casually in the air, brushes aside my growing panic. Our asylums, you say, are filled with those who would be penitent. It is then we tread the will of others into dust, or, in desperation, invoke the will of angels.

Again your body shape. The image swirls in silk. O the gentle caress of silk and nylon, the full pleasure of your mouth. A circle of silence. A cave, warm and dark. Now your subtle scent comes to me, a fragrance full of the August sea.

Before I was dead, I watched you and desired to play this game, to know the premonition behind the mask.

Before you were drowsy and bored, I longed to coax your hair and kiss your veiled eyes. Your slightly parted lips.

I dreamt you dressed in black silk and wore perfumes scented with the haunting sorrow of a thousand small deaths.

Walls build up around us, solid, rigid. We have come to admire this grotesque geometry. Each move adds a stone to the wall and slowly the maze grows. I know one of us will fail and the walls and corridors crumble. In this game, you say, we pay dearly for our daily temptations.

I plot every move carefully. I watch over all my men, each on his own path. Yet it is too confusing as different patterns unfold on the board, changing strategies each designed to win the game. I no longer distinguish my path, my plan, from yours. A labyrinth of scaffolds weaves in and out, out and in. Images stabbed through the eyes are branded on the mind behind. No move escapes your inspection. Painted birds sing from their hooded cages; fire scorches the earth. Are there rules? Was there a pact made before the beginning?

ᨑ

Our history is recorded only in moments of intense sobriety. We record the years without understanding, without question. The sun drops from a burning sky. Love is charred. Smoke, like wings, carries on the wind. Drunk, we weep for our lies, for those dead of emptiness.

Be gentle with your words that they may carry the weight of simple laughter.

Be gentle with your swords that they not cut the heart from strangers.

Listen, the winds of misfortune shed tears in the deserts that lie beyond the edge of this world. There, laughter is burdened by memory.

❧

I think of moving my power to the front, of using my queen, of sending out my knights to attack. So begins the slaughter, a light dusting of snow on the graves of the lost. Attack? I am uneasy with this power and wonder what blood mutiny drives us toward oblivion. The hour must be carefully chosen, otherwise your hands will close on my throat.

You, my love, would you have us as one? Stripped to the skin, I fear the violent light of this summer sun. Your tongue curls along your lips; your fingertips circle your thighs, slowly, moving outside time, beckoning.

I am floating toward ambush, trapped in the perfume of this dying day.

Can your fingers heal the wounds? Can the dawn awaken, like ripe fruit, without a scar?

Ask the birds as they compose a grammar of our love in the invisible skies.

ॐ

I would place my hand between your legs if I did not fear my tongue would lose the way of words. I would rejoice in my silence if I could hear you cry out in your wish to devour me.

The path is bordered by walls solid enough to conceal my passing. I have flashes of a breakthrough where in a previous time some unknown figure has escaped. Shadow figures move through stone; angels tremble before the savage calculations of twilight.

I know that one day I will suffer curiosity. Like everyone I also know the offspring, this creature of escape. If I am to free myself I have little doubt that I will stoop to carry the burden of this beast, imagination, and you, you will accuse me of committing suicide.

ða

Listen, we come to the feast, the midnight dance, dressed in funereal splendor.

I do not speak to you, nor you to me. In silence the game continues. Then for a brief moment the image of a hole appears and I flow out of the mould and escape. Free, I fly about madly, but soon recover my senses; I become bewildered, afraid. In the madness of fleeing I have lost my place of exit.

At first I feel almost dead. I search for another entrance, back through the walls. Has anyone else left the game? When I finally find others outside, they sit meditating on squares of concrete. For a while no one takes notice of me. After a time they speak, soft voices of the wind.

ta

O people, why do we dream of prisons? Why do we blush when the hibiscus flowers before our doubting eyes? Why do we let our desires roam the streets alone in darkness?

I would dance from window to window if you would
light a candle.

ta

And so these voices tell me that once outside I cannot
return. I will fight I tell them, smash the concrete.
Laughing, they say that each time a man is eliminated
the game comes closer to an end. At times a whole
square will fall away from the walls under the weight
of many men fleeing at once, in one place. I have left a
bruise on the wall, weakened a spot for the next man
to plunge through. The day will come when all the
walls will crumble. Fools, I yell, the game is eternal.
Shaking their heads and smiling, they tell me I alone
am the guilty architect of these dreams of escape. I
hear them all singing and laughing and soon we all
sing and laugh . . . a chorus of rejoicing which shakes
the walls . . .

There is hope I tell myself.

ﻪ

I am alone, running . . .

ﻪ

Perspiration rolls down my face. I look up the alley and see two figures glide by the entrance. Not a busy section of the city. Nowhere to lose myself. My lungs ache from running. I glance over my shoulder and barely miss colliding with two people who block my path. Moving quickly between parked cars, I cross the road. Farther down the street is another alley, swallowed up by the shade of tall bordering buildings. I undo my collar button. No one. Where are they? I jog down the narrow passage; a pain develops in my side. The end looks like a porthole glancing out over a calm sea. Shimmering outlines move by the exit. The cloth of my shirt sticks to my skin. White buildings rise into the heavens across the way from the opening. Shapes flow in a haze of cyclonic dust ascending on the rays of the sun. How I long to be in the country, sitting before a fire . . . watching the quiet fall of snow. Sweat now runs freely from my pores, into my eyes and mouth, brackish . . . this taste, the coolness of the sea. The ordeal is imminent. I burst into the white fire of an open street.

Assassins are rarely careless.

ॐ

I am stopped. I glance down to my hands which clasp tightly to my belly. A fluid drains over my fingers. I feel weak and warm. I look at the tired faces. Then I relax one hand and with the other pull out a bullet. The pain subsides . . . pours out of me. I sink to the pavement, kneeling as if in supplication.

My eyes open; I look into the enclosing faces. A man in uniform, a grey uniform, has taken charge of the crowd. I see a woman trying to get closer but the crowd stops her. Is it you?

Who, I wonder, in this time of fierce constellations, will sing our praises when the heart is cold?

Was it you who hired the hunters?

&

You cross your legs and, with the last shadow of torture, I am plunged out of dream. You place your skirt over your knees, deliberately. The graceful arc of your wrist, quick. The short flick up and, for a moment, I see the bare flesh of your thigh.

As I watch you, I know the way of mercy.

I expect you to speak. But the other, the voice of the other, is silent. Silent. When I shudder you merely raise yourself on one elbow and smile.

Was it then the city burst into flames? Was it then we wept for our loss of words?

I know an emptiness nothing can fill. Oblivion, you say. Under a crescent moon, I watch your hands, as if moving through water, caress the air. My desire rises with the swell of the sea.

Held in this moment, as you descend on me, a bird flies by my face. A great fluttering of wings stirs the air. As I lie there the earth beneath me is cool and moist. My tongue circles your breasts. Your lips enclose and bind me.

Slowly, turning, your long legs part and cut through the dark, scissor and enfold me. Layer upon layer, I enter the depths. Your body on fire.

Once you spoke of an endless and marvelous dying.

ॐ

To know nothing is divine mischief.

Is it not enough to know time hoards the shrouds?

❧

We remember how the ancients fled into corners to die, their bones resting against the walls.

O, how we wailed but kept the secret with our lives.

And O how we ignored the betrayers, those who told us to kiss our wives, our children; told us to embrace the earth, love the smell of the sea.

Why is it we seek the murderers?

Trapped in time, intent on the moments matter, we accumulate pleasure as if it had permanence, as if we were not the target of the assassins bullet. These faces persist, gather to witness the slow death of mirrors.

&

I lie back and close my eyes. I am walking from blackness into a garden. Black then white slowly blend into different shades. I open my eyes. All the colours unfold in a thunderclap of petals, roses and violets, marigolds and dahlias. The odour of earth fills my nostrils. I hear verse in a soft voice . . . your voice? I glide carefully through the garden which now opens into a valley far beyond the reach of my sight. I move toward a fountain, a bench. Before me there are men and women, naked, whose tears replenish the earth.

Who would lament this light that drives darkness to the other side of the sky;

who would lament the wind that plucks the harp;

and who, they ask, would turn his back on the beggar or not forgive the assassin his dagger?

❧

In the air there is a madness which emanates from these people. At first I am threatened by them but gradually I begin to see . . . to understand. Again I hear the soft voice reading poetry. It flows on the notes of a symphony. Fading, then rising, and once more fading. Your voice, I am certain now.

So, I welcome your song, and wait for you to live in me.

Is this the shape you choose? An elusive spirit. I want to run my fingers across your lips. Kiss the rise of your belly. Feel the heat of the sun in the weave of our shadows.

ᔰ

A wind blows through the open kitchen window; the curtains brush against my face. I run my hand over a days growth of beard. Slowly my eyes focus on the board and I see that its my move. I pass my hand over my shoulder and down my chest to my belly.

There is a lunacy behind this game that lies beyond the edge of the board. Even I can see that.

You are becoming unbearable. My shirt sticks to my stomach. The cloth is damp and my skin recoils from the wetness. How? How has it happened?

As I look up a small triangle of black silk slides over your thighs. Often I have noticed that your legs are as smooth as your breasts. Yet never has your skin appeared so soft and white. A cool nakedness.

You stretch your arms into the air and spread your fingers, reaching back, back, opening.

&

Truth forces itself to your lips, red and distilled. You smile. Gestures as simple as these mediate between stones.

We embrace only when we deny that we belong to our own longing.

My eyes focus away from the heat waves which ripple in the lamp light. We drink the last of the wine and sit looking out. It is late and the night very still and quiet. I think of my day in the city, in the office. Of the lingering faces of stone.

ॐ

Too soon mirrors betray old desires. Whispers of death, clothed in the affections of beauty. Beyond the garden we hear voices wailing. We sense something nameless brush past us, but we know there is no turning back. We listen to the beat of our hearts. We taste these affirmations of youth, of the new body.

ॐ

To live divinely is to embrace simple joys; to partner the holy grace of moonlight. To live out of time, beyond the brief darkness of dreams, is to court demons.

Listen, walk the streets through this city as if the jackal
snapped at your heels.

☙

What we heard was not the vision.
What we saw was not the trumpet of Jericho.
What we tasted was not the fragrance of the morning
sun, an open orange blossom.
What we smelled was not the salt of your thighs, the
song on your red lips.
What we felt was not the end.

Your hand reaches for mine; you wait until the music falls silent before you beckon me to follow. I rise. You lead me from the kitchen. The rooms are cooler now. We crawl into the white tangle of sheets. I no longer think of snow. Is it safe to touch . . . to love? At dawn the sea is still. Can it be, as a bird soars where it might have been, in the fullness of a blue sky, that you have entered my soul? I stare at the walls. White sheets, white bodies, white paper.

ABOUT THE AUTHOR

Ron Smith was born in Vancouver, B.C. in 1943. He studied at the University of British Columbia and later, in England, at the University of Leeds. His stories and poems have been published in magazines in Australia, Canada, England, Jugoslavia and the United States. In 1974 he founded the publishing house Oolichan Books and served as its publisher until 1994. Between 1987 and 1990, he was the Fiction Editor for Douglas & McIntyre. He has also served as editor on award-winning books from other Canadian publishers. Over the past twenty-five years he has given numerous readings and workshops, most recently at the Marlborough Arts Festival, Wiltshire, England, and at the Festival of the Written Arts in Sechelt, B.C. Since 1971 he has taught English and Creative Writing at Malaspina University-College in Nanaimo. He lives with his family in Lantzville on Vancouver Island.